EXPLORE
Yourself
with 100+ Keys

EXPLORE Yourself

with 100+ Keys

Authored by

VEERA S SURAMPUDI

Penman Books

Office No. 303, Kumar House Building,
D Block, Central Market, Opp PVR Cinema,
Prashant Vihar, Delhi 110085, India
Website: www.penmanbooks.com
Email: publish@penmanbooks.com

First Published by Penman Books 2019
Copyright © Veera S Surampudi 2019
All Rights Reserved.

Title: Explore Yourself with 100+ Keys
Price: ₹300 | $15
ISBN: 978-16-59082-74-6

Dedication

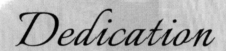

This book be dedicated to
my parents Chandra Rao, Jagadeswari,
my wife Aruna and my children Sahiya and Hrishik!

Special Thanks to Vincent Smith,
Bala Bathula and Nehal Patil who helped me in the

Quotes Phrase formation, Author Biography and
Introduction page Presentation!

And finally, Thanks to everyone
on my publishing team!

It's not easy to
change a mindset.
But it is not difficult to
change if you want to live in
the global world!

If you don't make friends that
is fine, but never
make enemies!

Everything happens
for a reason. It might
be good or bad!
Understand it, accept it and
move on in life's Journey

Clarity is needed for any kind of Effort. If no clarity, effort will never turn to results like ocean water drained with a small bucket!

> Good things happen slowly!
> Bad things happen quickly!

"Thinking about beloved people is not a weakness, it's a strength. Thinking about little known/ small favored people is not strength, it's a weakness!

Some people always hate their own people for their inner problems instead of finding the root cause of the problem!

Even if it takes longer, non-forceable correction is a better choice than forceful correction to fix mistakes!

> Find where you lost
> instead of Losing hope!

We should be chosen
Entertainment, not vice versa!

> Beliefs should allow change for improvement, not the opposite!

Life means live until death
finds you. No matter what kind
of troubles you are facing.
You must lead your life until
the end!

> Mean people criticize you, Narrow minded people scrutinize you, Open minded people will admire you when you do something meaningful!

Believe in yourself, not others! At the same time, your belief should build with consciousness, not with materialistic thoughts!

> People with low self-esteem will pull you down to where they are. Don't suffer without understanding their intentions!

Live close to where
your value is countable,
not your wealth!

The Right mind always makes the right decisions even in angry moments!

Interest turns to weakness
when you don't have control
of your mind!

> Don't stick to the concept of young or old!
> Stick to the concept of healthy or unhealthy!

The Combination of Patience and good planning will always give good results!

Respect yourself!
If you don't respect yourself,
no one will respect you!

Get a hold of yourself, not others, to succeed in life!

Be happy! If you can't,
at least make others happy!

Don't look at everything
from your point of view.
If you want to understand
density of an issue, you must
walk a mile in their shoes!

A Competitive spirit will make you more independent!
A Competitive mind will make you more dependent!

Everything has a turning point! Wait for your turning point with positivity to resolve issues

"Don't go by words without understand a situation! Meaning of words will vary from situation to situation and time to time!"

If you don't accept your own mistakes and weaknesses you will never grow!

> Fear makes you helpless,
> even the situation around
> you not that bad!
> Don't fear, be clear!

A pre-occupied mind doesn't allow you to understand new things

Interest is the key factor
to achieve anything!
When you compare interest
with other things, all are
secondary

Your Beauty lies in your thought process, not in your physical appearance!

When you don't have a path
to reach even Opportunities
are available, go by your own
instincts to find the path!

First understand yourself
if you want to understand
others!

You have a right to walk out
from a Relationship.
But you never have a right to
walk out from Responsibility
as a human being!

The "I don't know" attitude is better than the "I know it" attitude!

> If you are in the dark, you can switch on the Light to eliminate darkness!
> But if your mind in the dark, there is no way to switch the Light on in your life until you realize yourself!

Comparison is not just mental weakness,it slowly takes away your peace too!

Inspiration is a cool thing!
Imitation is not!

Easy to attract Negativity when you have a dependent mentality!

Until you understand, it's a Myth! Once you understand, it's a Truth!

Language is a
Communication channel to
understand content, not a
measurement for Knowledge!

Believing your dreams
are more powerful than
Achieving them!

Your Anger is your Enemy!
Your calmness is your
Strength!

" You can finish your graduation in 4yrs, you can finish your PhD in 7yrs.
But to understand yourself it takes a Life time! "

Make your Eye 'Sharp-Eyed'
to see what is in front of you,
not what you feel inside
of you!

Self-Discipline is a powerful
weapon to lead a life in
the right direction!

Believing in yourself all the time is one of the toughest tasks when you have a Balanced mind

You have the choice to help others or not, but you do not have the choice or right to harm others!

Generally, we think actions
will tell better than words
about personality.
But small incidents and
reactions will tell about
personality when compare
with actions!

Assuming others are so lowly is worse than assuming themselves are so high & mighty

Some people are born to suffer. Not because of their physical disability, because of their mental disability (Greed, jealous and comparison to others)

Clouds will disappear slowly,
but the Sky will remain
the same!
Attraction will melt slowly,
but real beauty of heart will
remain the same

> In this world people think others are competitors. In reality, you are the competitor of yourself, not others!

Getting good advice at the
right time is the Luckiest
thing in the world when the
person is at the confusion
state of mind!

> People can't see the things in the dark! But some people can't see the things even they are in the light, due to darkness of mind!

Escapist is a more relaxed
person in the present.
But, more frustrated person
in the future!

What you are
expecting is not life,
What you are accepting
is a life!

Success will create
one successful option
most of the time!
But failure will create multiple
options to explore and
succeed in a life!

Some people deeply suffer
with false prestige and
superior assumptions about
themselves!
Do not knock on their door
when you realize their nature!

Don't feel like a slap on someone's face who has humiliated you badly! Feel like slapping your own face, because you allowed them to humiliate you!

Fortune means, not to just have a money in a life! Fortune means, to be blessed with positive people around you!

> Emotions are key elements in human day to day life! Emotions are generated by the mind, not by you. Keep watch as a gate keeper until it melts down. Do not become that emotion at all

 God never gives
everything to anyone!
If you don't realize that,
you will never be
happy in life

> Remove negative segments of thoughts with positive Aroma to live in a happy moment

Hate will destroy your
peace, not others

Helping others is a very
good quality without
expecting anything.
But, be sure your good
quality is not being
misused by others ..

Honest admiration not just
makes others happy, it makes
yourself feel better too!

Think about big things to
build your future!
But live with small things to
build inner happiness!

Hate will develop when a
person has an insecure
mindset!

Your life need not be inspirational for someone to lead their life in the best way. But your life shouldn't be a bad example for others!

 Don't allow someone's words
to lead your decision!
At the same time, don't
neglect other's words
as well

Live in the moment! Not in the past, not in the future! But at the same time mold your future by learning from the past

Love is one kind of emotion generated by the mind, not you.
Learn how to control your mind when the emotion dominates you!

If you want to be real
member of a household,
stop thinking with mind and
start thinking with heart!

When we wear shoes,
we don't know how
hard the surface is.
We only know once we
lost a shoe in the middle
of the walk!

> Nature will play with our minds according to human-nature Relationship!
> If you can't give something to others, your mind won't be able to take it from others due to Nature's force

Some people don't have
anything to do other
than self-interest!
If your life is stuck with them,
you never see sunshine in
your life until you realize
yourself!

Update yourself,
not commodities if you
want to live up to date!

> People come and go in life, but your own people neither come nor go easily

In the real world, people get recognition based on where they stand-up, not based on what they are!

Being an open-minded person is always good. But, try to avoid having conversations with pre-occupied people. Otherwise surely you will suffer with their judgmental thoughts!

> Quality of cloth and human mentality both are the same. We will know only after usage!

> Rights & Responsibilities
> are powerful weapons to
> guide human life!
> If you misfire those weapons,
> your future will be scattered
> Instead of Built!

Forgive others to
correct themselves.
Do not forgive again, if the
same mistake is repeated!

if self-confidence comes
with clarify of mind, that
will be eternal.
If self-confidence comes
with a cloudy mind, it will
slowly disappear like clouds!

Selfish people are might
be winning their desires,
not the people!

> Sexual attached love is replaceable. Non-Sexual attached love is non-replaceable!

Struggle has to dissolve your
issues to achieve goals, not
to dissolve your goals!

Don't suffer long when you are stuck with an emotion or feeling! Suffer for a period and come out from that emotion or feeling forever

Success is not a milestone
for life's journey!
Success is stepping stone
for new adventure in life's
journey!

The 'Superiority in Inferiority Complex' is worse than the 'Superiority Complex'!

"Even with thousands of people around you, only few will be with you for a life time. If you can't identify them, you will become alone at one point in time!

> Un processed love and
> half cooked food both
> are the same.
> Both results are end up with
> stomach pain, nothing else!

Comparing yourself with others is an Amateur thing! If you find at least one person to compare yourself in your lifetime, that would be miraculous

Your perception depends on
how you feel inside of you,
not a thing which is existing
there!

Happiness is an output
of joy, share it!
Pain is an input of your
struggle, deal it!

If you are looking for happiness in others, you will get peanuts!
If you are looking for happiness inside of you, will get donuts/dessert

> Change has to start from you!
> Not from others, don't wait...

Some people never get
success, reason the always
focus on results,
not on goal/task!

Focus on your work,
not output!

Find Satisfaction in
what you are doing,
not in what you gain!

Live with Values,
not with items!

If you know how to grow and trim plants, you will know how to lead life too! The reason being both depends on the same philosophy!

No need to know what others think in general!
But you should be capable to know what others think about you!

"
Meaningful silence is a
powerful weapon.
It will help others to realize
their mistakes and correct
them!
"

> If fear comes from inside,
> it will turn as greedy
> and selfish!
> If fear comes from outside,
> it will turn to prejudice!

Relationship is a life. It can be
with human or nature!

You can't control someone's actions, but you can control their actions with your reaction!

"
Money will come and go!
When we lose money,
the impact is great.
so, try to live with money,
not just for money

Some people never fail in life, because they never crossed their safe zone!

> If you share your pain with the right person, pain will resolve. If you share your pain with the wrong person, you will dissolve, not the pain!

Fail one hundred times to achieve goals in life, but never end life with failure!

Cleverness doesn't just depend on Intelligence and knowledge, it depends on how you apply it

You no need to share your own mistakes with others. Must be realize your own mistakes at the end of the day if you want to correct yourself.

> Don't dis-respect those who asked a favor from you. Respect them, reason being they valued a lot.

> " Even a pair of shoes will fit well to your feet, if the order was mismatched, the foot never fits into the shoe. In the same token, even you have everything if you don't maintain order, happiness never gets into your life! "

No one is a born with
perfection!
It will build in you day-by-day
by correcting your
own mistakes!

Fake people act according to your wishes just to gain something, but Real people not!

Questioning yourself is a good habit when you don't understand something! Sometimes your own subconscious will give an answer for your question at one point of life's journey!

Even if you have done
100 good things,
one bad thing can follow
you for a lifetime!

Follow someone until you learn, then allow others to follow you to learn...!

Don't neglect the person who is in inside of you who will always stay within you

"Love and hate are two emotions generated by the mind!
Your lifestyle depends on which emotion is dominates your mind

 Balance of thought not
just depends on your vision
and perception.
It depends on how much
you understand yourself

Live the way you want!
But, make sure you are aware
of barriers and boundaries
of freedom!

> One of the toughest things
> in the world is, understand
> yourself!

"
Don't blame others for your mistakes even they are involved in the decision making, blame yourself for not being aware of the consequences of your decision!

Show the anger on your own people to correct them, not to release your frustration!

Live with money,
but not live for money!

Pain and joy are all
a part of life's journey.
when you get a pain, feel and
deal the same way with joy.
Feel it and solve it!

When people fail to understand you, don't try to prove your innocence. If they need your presence, they will get to know you!

Age is related to the body, not mind or soul. Use your experience of Age to elevate yourself, not to degrade yourself with Age Syndrome

An Escapist blame other
for his problems!
An Optimist never blames
others for his problems!

Illusions makes humans
stay away from reality.
Self-analyzation is the best
practice to expel illusion

Life is like Train journey!
People come and go in every
stop, but your people always
will be with you until end of
your journey

Sometimes strength will turn to weakness! When you don't realize the thin line between those two stages, you will be miserable

It's not possible to think and talk when we are angry, we can control anger by responding instead of reacting!

If you want to be role model,
try to avoid doing things
which you don't like in others!

"

Even if they are good people,
maintain distance if you don't
sync up. That's not only good
for you, it's good for them
too!

"

"Those who can understand
what is in front of them,
are the most successful
people in the world!

Fact is one, but perceptions are 1000. If your perception is nearest to Fact, that means your mind is clear and focused

"If you neglect your roots and customs, you will get lot of freedom to do what you like! By the time you realize your mistakes, your life will be out of your hands!"

> People won't change.
> But priorities will change
> from time to time!
> When priorities change,
> other's perception will
> change on you, even you
> are the same person

> Any kind of Emotion needs to be evaluated with Responsibility. If you apply that, you will never get stuck with any Emotion for a long period of time!

> If you don't understand the root cause of your pain, pain will make you a slave! If you understand, pain will purify your mind & soul!

How long you live is not the
matter! How effectively you
live is the matter!

If you don't understand your roots, you can't predict your future!

Don't try to trap someone.
Be careful if you do,
your mind will make you a
trap without knowing you!

Directly or indirectly, someone can be your enemy. But, never be an enemy of yourself in any situation no matter what it is!

Too much freedom will absorb your future freedom!

It is easy to judge others,
but the difficulty lies in
understanding others!

Agree or Disagree, doesn't matter! You and inside of you fight like day and night until you become inside of you!

> What others did for
> you doesn't matter!
> What you do for
> others matter

Made in the USA
San Bernardino, CA
07 February 2020